MUZIO CLEMENTI

(1752–1832)

SIX SONATINAS, OPUS 36

for the piano

Edited by Keith Snell

D0128703

Contents

MUZIO CLEMENTI (1752-1832) was born in Rome, the capital city of Italy. He was born four years before Mozart and died five years after Beethoven. During his lifetime, Clementi was very famous and is still considered one of the most important men in the history of piano music.

Clementi's father encouraged Muzio to begin music lessons when he was very young. He learned to play the piano and the organ, to sing and to compose. When he was fourteen years old, Clementi gave a piano recital in Rome that impressed an English gentleman so much that he arranged to have Clementi move to England to study music with the finest English teachers. After six years of study in London, Clementi gave his debut concert. It was very successful. He gave more concerts in England and also performed in other cities such as Paris, Munich and Vienna.

For the rest of his life, Clementi lived in England and continued to give piano concerts. He also composed and was a piano teacher. Many of the best young English musicians were his students. He also was successful in business and owned a piano manufacturing company and a music publishing company.

Among his many well-known works for the piano are *The Art of Playing on the Piano-Forte* and *Gradus ad Parnassum*. One of his most successful works is the *Six Sonatinas, Op. 36*. The well-deserved popularity of these sonatinas is due to their musical charm and the excellent material they provide for learning about classical sonata playing.

All pieces in this edition are in their original form, with dynamics, slurs, and articulation marks added by the editor as suggestions for musical interpretation. For supplementary study, a recording is available on compact disc (GP379CD) performed by pianist Diane Hidy. Ms. Hidy's performance is closely matched to the editorial markings as a practical example for students.

The painting on the cover of this book is by Pal Szinyei Merse (1825-1920).

ISBN 0-8497-6194-8

Sonatina in C major
Opus 36, No. 1

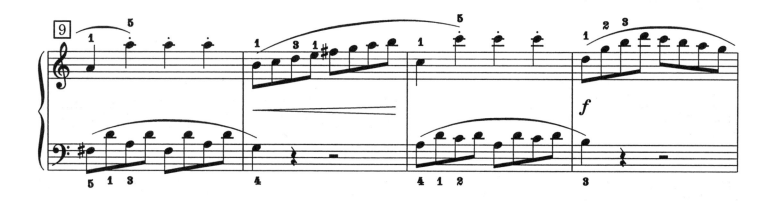

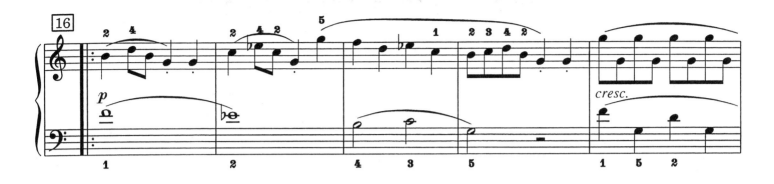

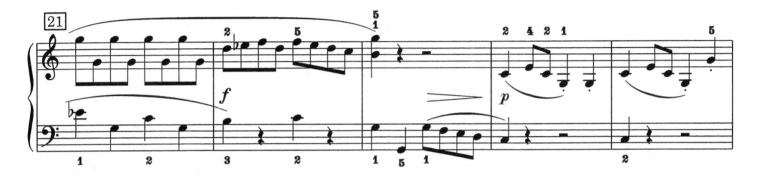

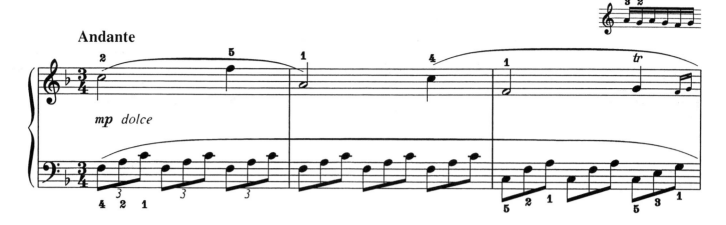

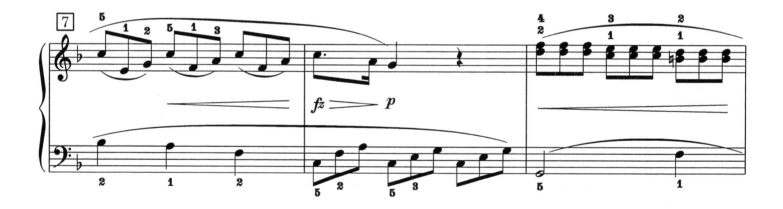

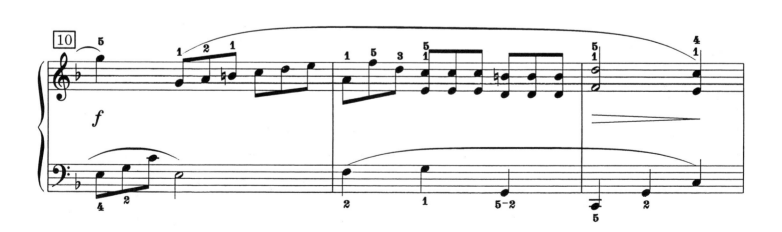

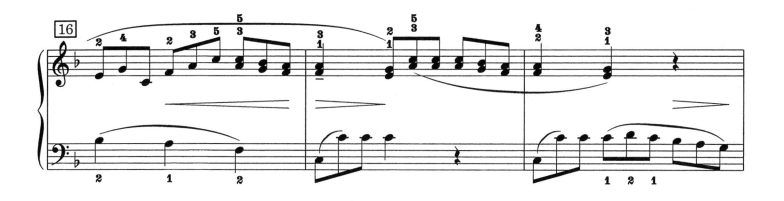

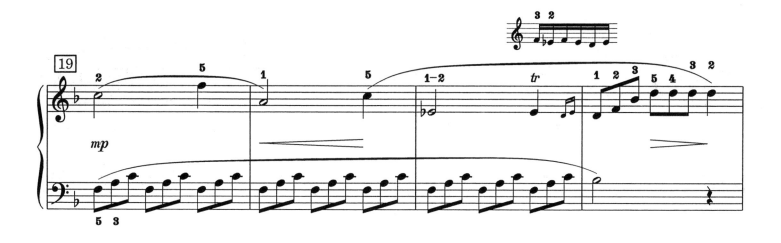

6

Rondo

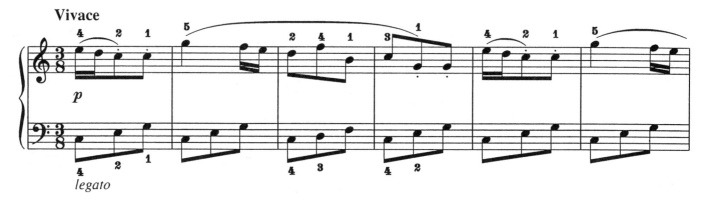

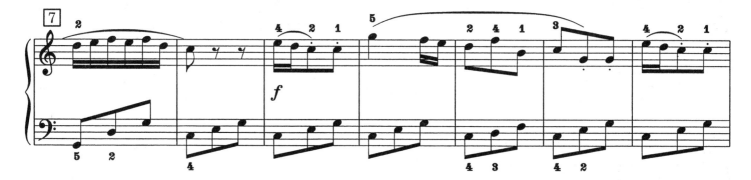

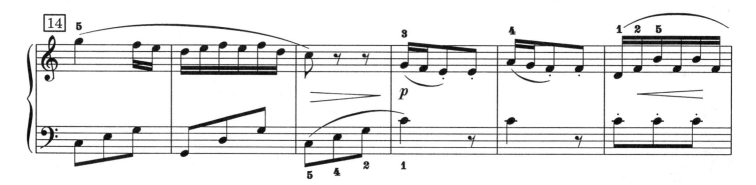

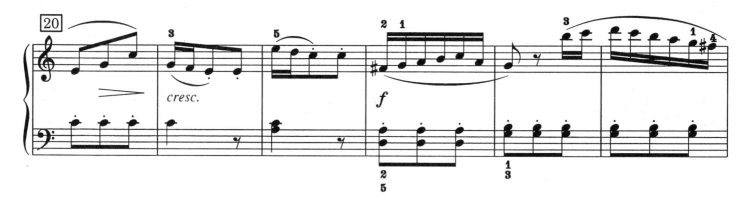

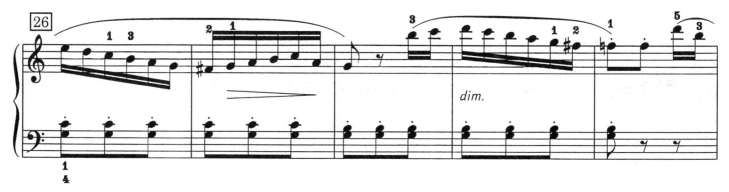

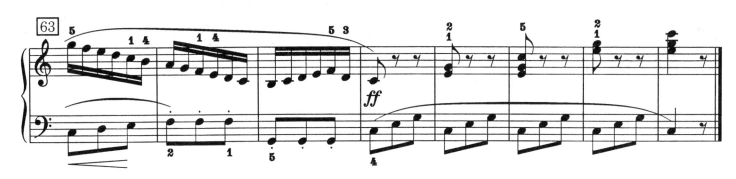

SONATINA IN G MAJOR
Opus 36, No. 2

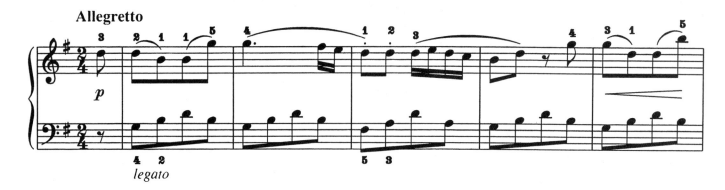

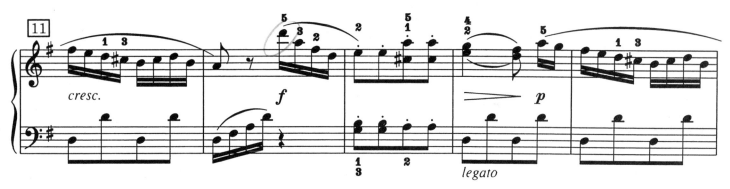

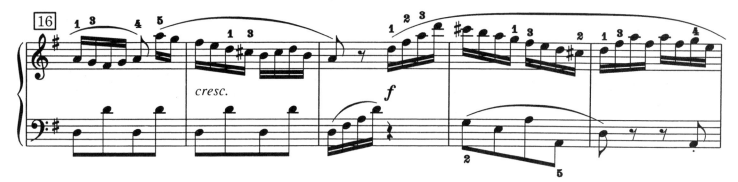

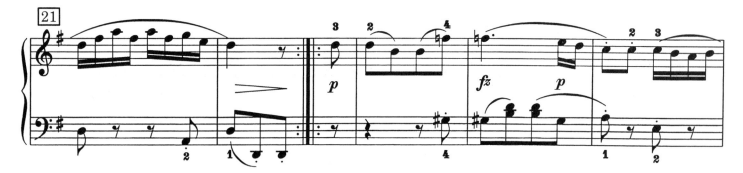

Allegretto

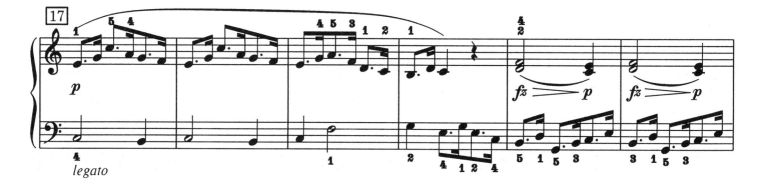

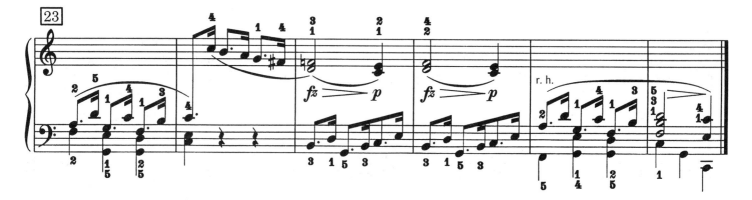

Rondo

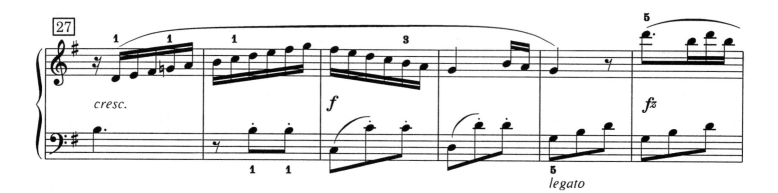

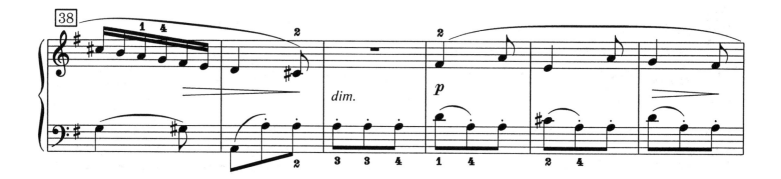

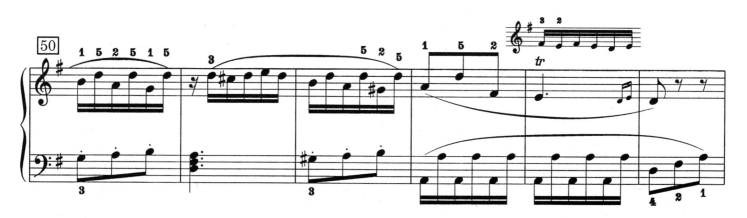

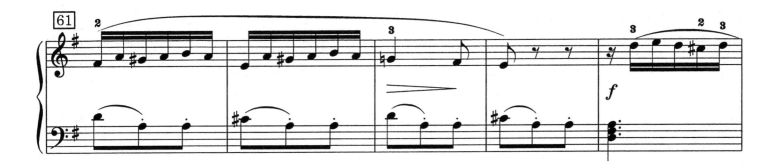

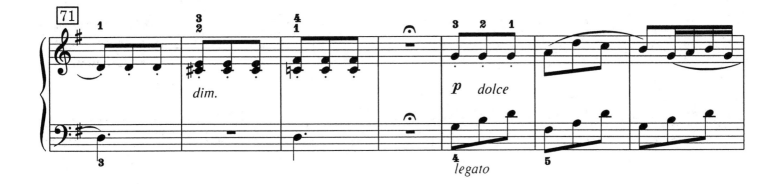

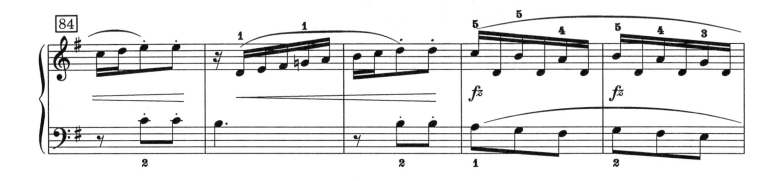

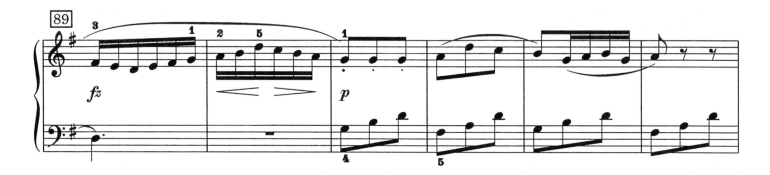

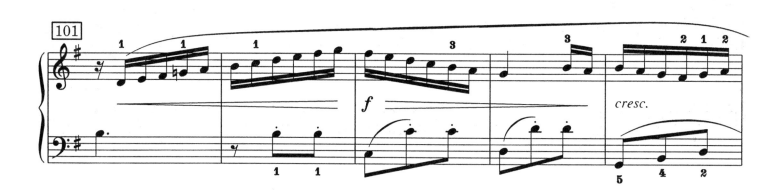

SONATINA IN C MAJOR

Opus 36, No. 3

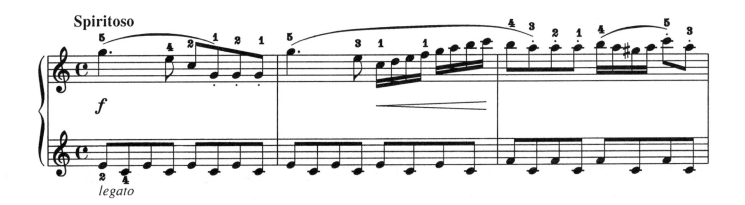

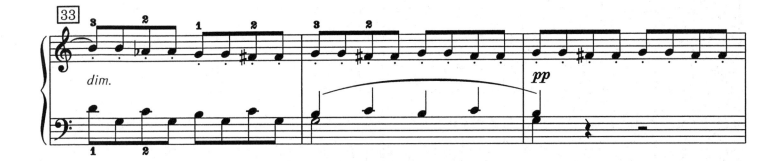

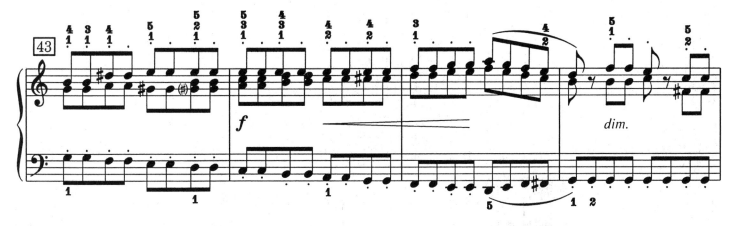

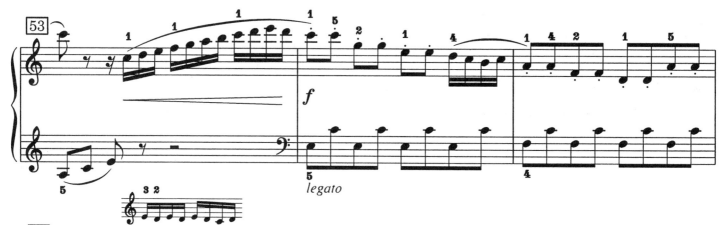

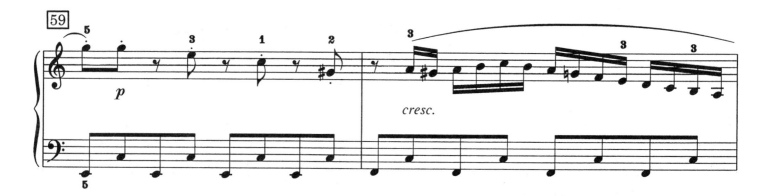

Un poco adagio

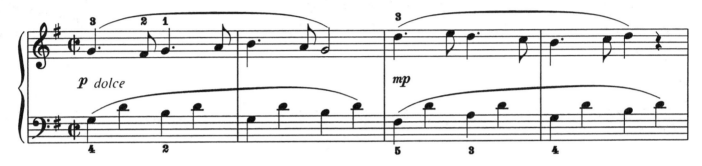

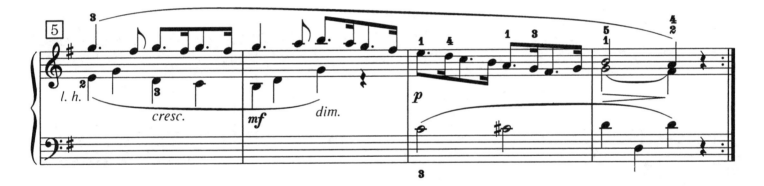

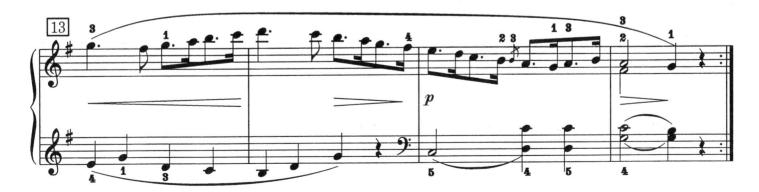

Allegro

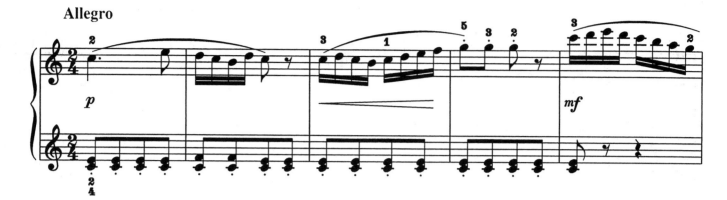

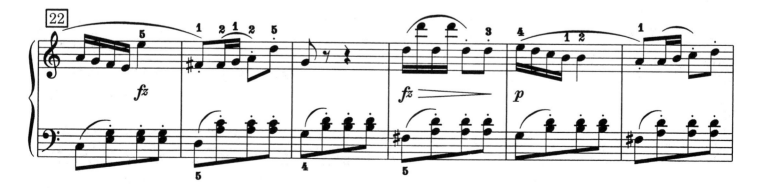

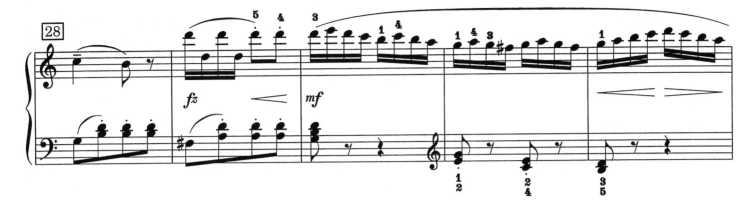

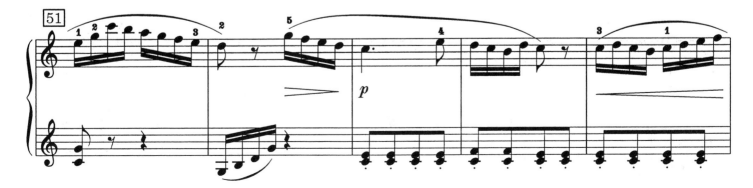

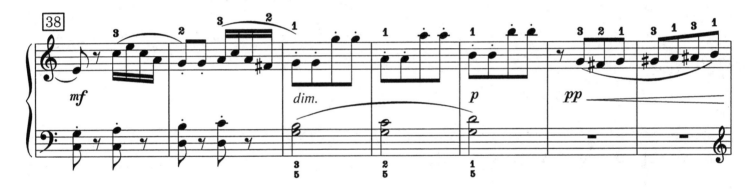

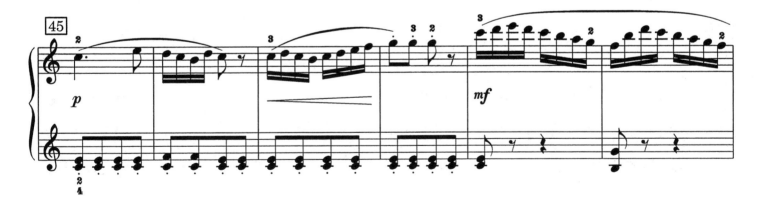

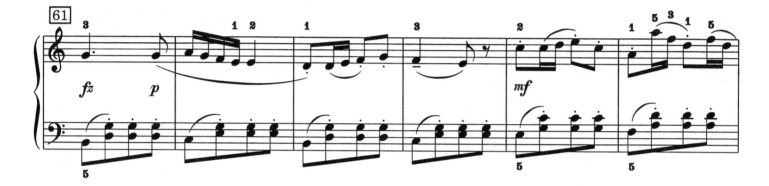

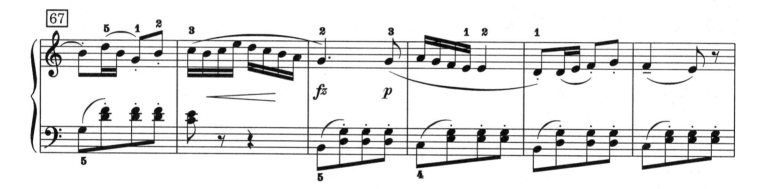

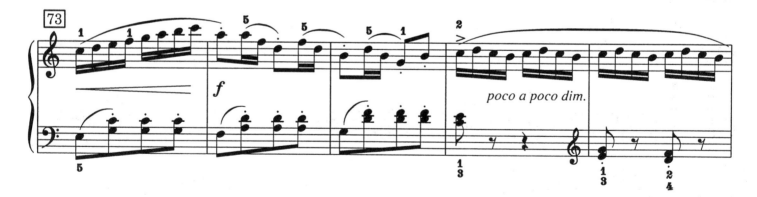

SONATINA IN F MAJOR
Opus 36, No. 4

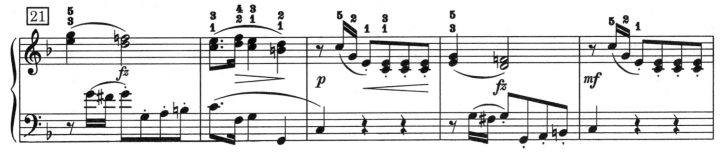

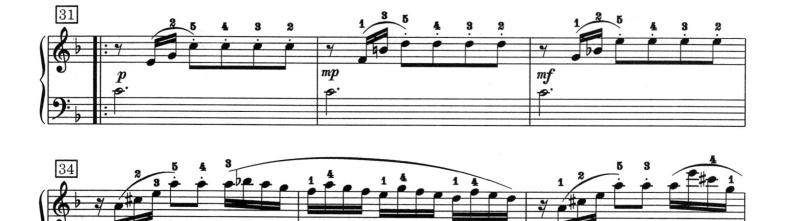

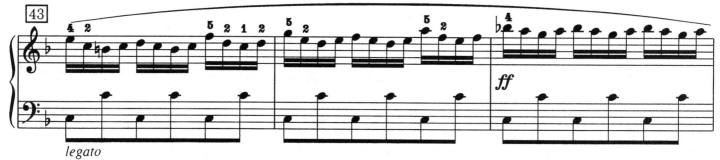

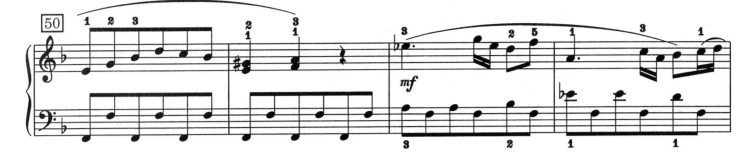

Andante con espressione

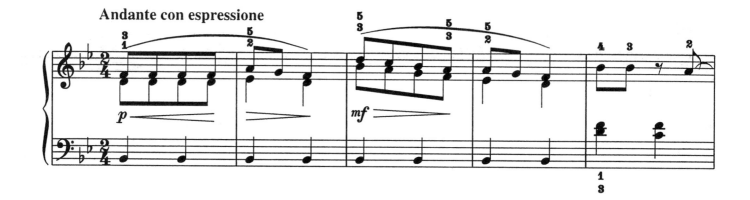

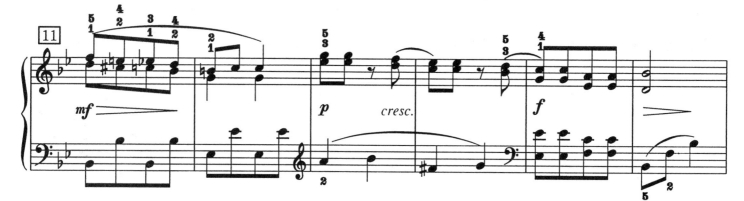

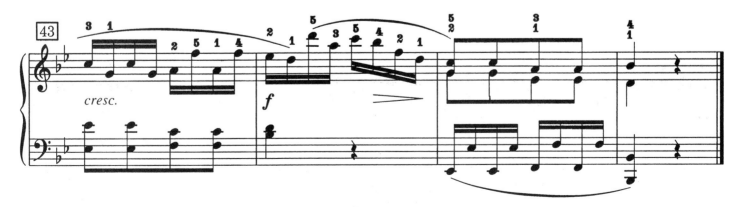

Rondo

Allegro vivace

SONATINA IN G MAJOR
Opus 36, No. 5

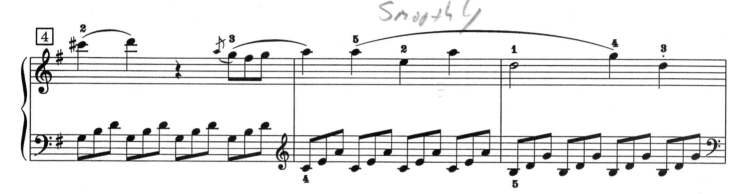

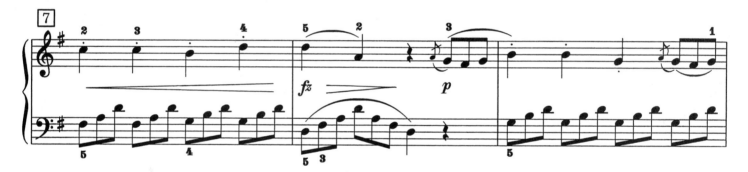

6/3

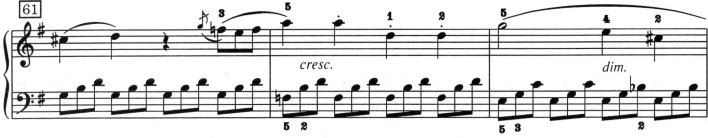

Air Suisse

Allegro moderato

Rondo

Allegro di molto

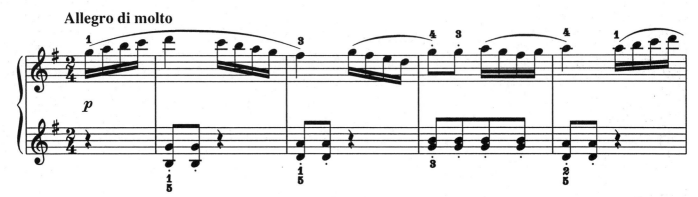

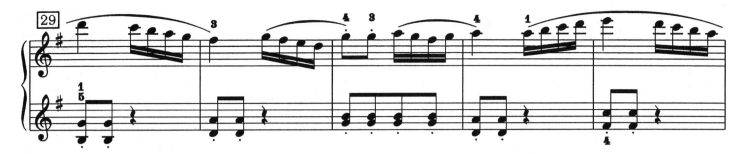

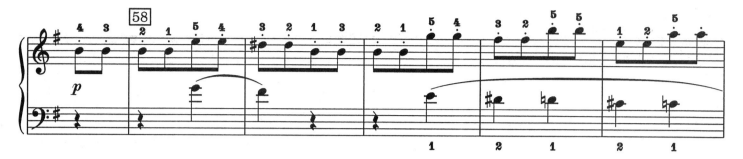

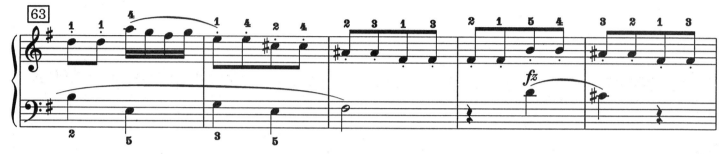

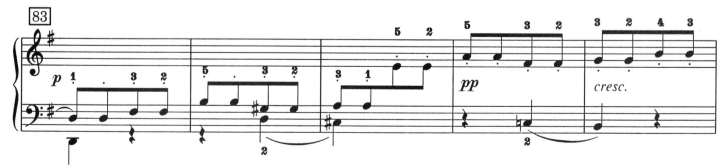

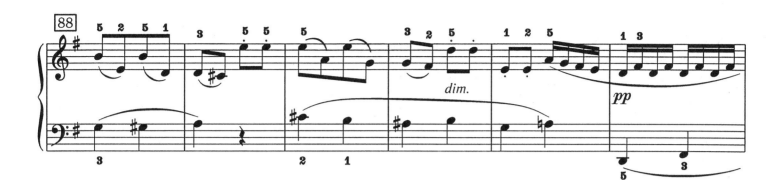

D. C. al Fine

SONATINA IN D MAJOR

Opus 36, No. 6

Allegro con spirito

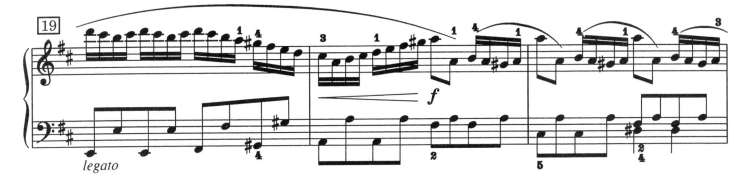

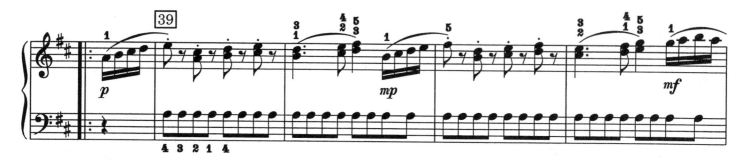

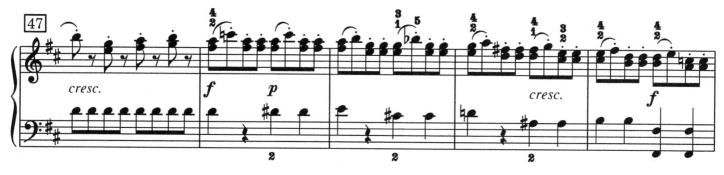

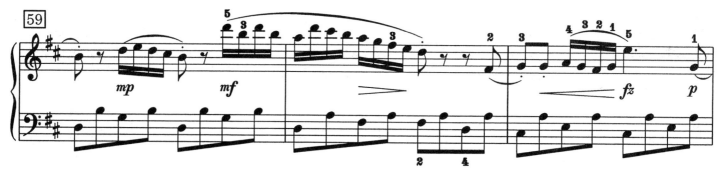

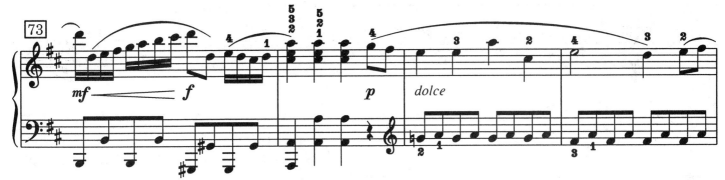

Rondo
Allegretto spiritoso

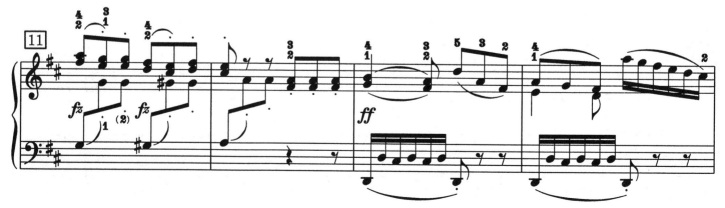

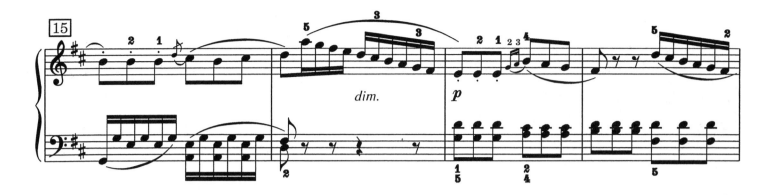

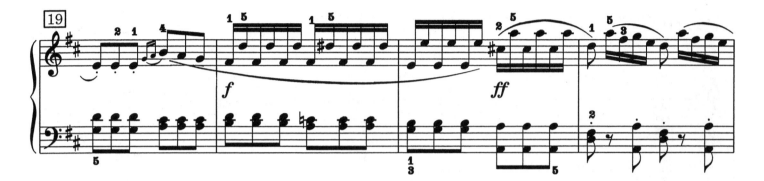

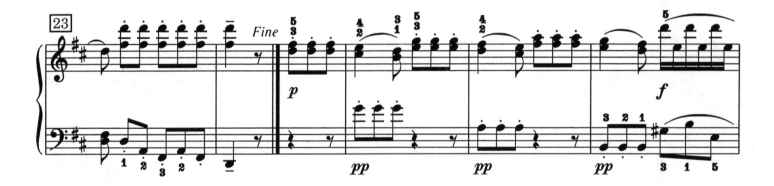

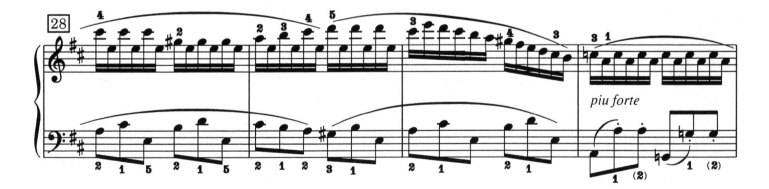

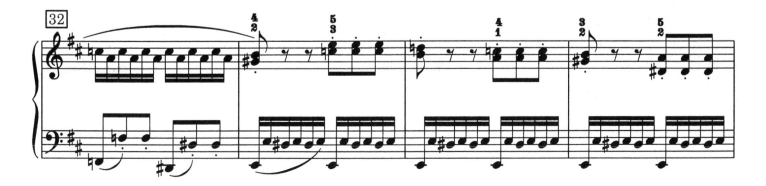

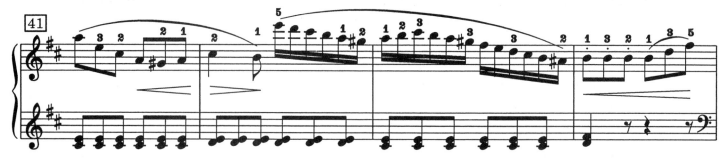

SONATINA FORM

A SONATINA is a short sonata. Sonatinas provide excellent music to play before studying longer, more complicated sonatas. Many first movements are based on a form called *sonata-allegro*, which was commonly used during the classical period of music writing (1770-1820).

A sonatina or sonata may have one, two or three movements. If there is more than one movement, they are usually contrasting in tempo and character.

First movements usually have this form *(sonata-allegro)*:
1. EXPOSITION
   a) first theme
   b) second theme (usually in a contrasting key)
   c) closing theme (optional)

2. DEVELOPMENT
   Themes are presented in new keys and sometimes new material is added.

3. RECAPITULATION
   a) first theme
   b) second theme
   c) closing theme (optional)

Second movements are usually written in three parts, or *ternary form* (ABA):
A. first theme
B. second theme
A. first theme

Third movements are often written in *rondo* form:
A. first theme
B. second theme
C. third theme
A. first theme
B. second theme
Coda (optional)